GEARED FOR GROWTH BIBLE STUDIES

THE DRAMA OF REVELATION

A STUDY IN REVELATION

BIBLE STUDIES TO IMPACT THE LIVES OF ORDINARY PEOPLE

Written by Dorothy Russell

The Word Worldwide

CHRISTIAN FOCUS

For details of our titles visit us on our website
www.christianfocus.com

ISBN 1-84550-020-2

Copyright © WEC International

10 9 8 7 6 5 4 3 2 1

Published in 2005 by
Christian Focus Publications Ltd, Geanies House,
Fearn, Tain, Ross-shire, IV20 ITW, Scotland
and
WEC International, Bulstrode, Oxford Road,
Gerrards Cross, Bucks, SL9 8SZ

Cover design by Alister MacInnes

Printed and bound by Bell & Bain, Glasgow

CONTENTS

QUESTIONS AND NOTES

ANSWER GUIDE

PREFACE

GEARED FOR GROWTH

'Where there's LIFE there's GROWTH:
Where there's GROWTH there's LIFE.'

WHY GROW a study group?

Because as we study the Bible and share together we can

- learn to combat loneliness, depression, staleness, frustration, and other problems
- get to understand and love each other
- become responsive to the Holy Spirit's dealing and obedient to God's Word

and that's GROWTH.

How do you GROW a study group?

- Just start by asking a friend to join you and then aim at expanding your group.
- Study the set portions daily (they are brief and easy: no catches).
- Meet once a week to discuss what you find.
- Befriend others, both Christians and non-Christians, and work away together

see how it GROWS!

WHEN you GROW ...

This will happen at school, at home, at work, at play, in your youth group, your student fellowship, women's meetings, mid-week meetings, churches and communities,

you'll be REACHING THROUGH TEACHING.

INTRODUCTORY STUDY

This study is based throughout on the book by Michael Wilcock (TVP), reprinted under the title *The Message of Revelation (IVP 1989)*.

Leaders should certainly try to obtain a copy of this book, as it gives much detail and explanation that cannot be included in a study such as this.

The introduction to Revelation is found in 1:1-8. The rest of the text is divided into eight scenes:

Scene 1	1:9–3:22	Seven letters to churches
Scene 2	4:1–8:1	Seven seals opened
Scene 3	8:2–11:18	Seven trumpets sounded
Scene 4	11:19–15:4	Seven visions of cosmic conflict
Scene 5	15:5–16:21	Seven bowls poured out
Scene 6	17:1–19:10	Seven words of justice
Scene 7	19:11–21:8	Seven visions of ultimate reality
Scene 8	21:9–22:21	Seven final revelations

The reason for these eight scenes emerges when we ask ourselves each time: 'What does John see next? Where does the next scene of action take place?' This is what we find:

1. 1:12 'And when I turned I saw seven golden lampstands....'
2. 4:1 '... there before me was a door standing open in heaven. And the voice said ... "Come up here ...."'
3. 8:2 (After the silence in heaven) 'I saw the seven angels ....'
4. 11:19 'Then God's temple in heaven was opened ....'
5. 15:5 ... in heaven the temple, that is, the tabernacle of the 'Testimony, was opened.' (The Good News Bible calls this the 'Tent of God's presence'.)
6. 17:1, 3 'One of the seven angels ... said to me, "Come...". Then the angel carried me away in the Spirit into a desert.'
7. 19:11 'I saw heaven standing open ....'
8. 21:9, 10 'One of the seven angels ... said to me, "Come ...". And he carried me away in the Spirit to a mountain ....'

OUR WONDERFUL GOD
Which do you prefer? To read a good book, or to watch a good movie on TV or DVD? We all

have our own preferences. But when a friend tells you about a terrific movie he or she has seen, and tries to describe it to you, doesn't it set your imagination running?

It's a little bit like that with the book of Revelation. John is describing what he *saw*, God's great *visual aid*, and if we take time to listen to him carefully, we too will feel the excitement and catch the vision. Not only that, but the Holy Spirit promises that we will receive a special blessing (1:3).

Throughout the centuries:

> Stories have been communicated –
> first by word of mouth,
> then through the printed word,
> and now by television and movies.

> God has communicated –
> through His incarnate Word, the Lord Jesus,
> through His written word,
> and in Revelation, through pictures we can 'see'.

Have you tried reading this book before, and become bogged down in the imagery and symbolism? Many people think it has nothing to say to us in this day and age. But this is not so. Let us pray that the Lord will really open our eyes as we study together, so that we will hear the Word, and take to heart what is written (1:3).

Read and discuss chapter 1:1-3.
> Who is the real author of this book?
> For whom were these future events being revealed?
> Who wrote down what he saw?
> Who are the ones who can expect a blessing?
> What makes it an urgent message for us today? (22:12, 20)

Now read verses 4-8.
> Who were the first people to receive this letter?
> Can you find the Trinity mentioned in verses 4 and 5?
> Find out all you can about Jesus from verses 5-7.
> Which of these descriptions of Jesus thrills you most?

Look up two strands of prophecy about Jesus in Daniel 7:13 and Zechariah 12:10, and see how they came together in Revelation 1:7 (Also Matt. 24:30).

Pause for a moment and reflect on all that is implied in Revelation 1:8. Then look up these references:

Exodus 3:13, 14; Isaiah 40:21-28; 44:6; Revelation 4:8; 21:6; 22:13.

Is your God too small? Stretch your minds and share with each other your concept of what God is like.

* * *

When you go to the theatre and are shown to your seat in all the bustle and excitement before the show, isn't there a tremendous sense of pleasurable anticipation? You sit down and open your program. Perhaps you are familiar with some of the actors. Then the lights dim, the overture begins, and all is in readiness for the curtain to go up. What an exciting moment!

This is the point we are at in our study of Revelation. We have come here, opened the Book, glanced at the divine characters with whom we are familiar, and the curtain is now ready to go up for Scene I of the drama.

As we look at these chapters, we will 'see' the drama that John saw on the stage of his mind, and each of the eight scenes will be played with the background music of the words of Jesus,

'Behold I am coming soon.
Yes, I am coming soon.'

* * *

In what ways do you, personally, praise and worship the Lord? Be honest. Is it only when you are in church that you sing praises to Him? Do you ever praise Him aloud in your daily Quiet Time? Try it!

We *praise* God for *what He has done.*
We *worship* Him for *who He is.*

Try speaking aloud your worship and adoration of Him as you pray at home. This could open up a whole new dimension of prayer for you. Each week we shall take away some special verses to help us to draw closer to the Lord in our own personal times of worship.

This week, use Revelation 1:5b and 6 every day, saying: 'To You ...' in place of 'To Him ...'

STUDY 1

SCENE 1: SEVEN LETTERS

QUESTIONS

DAY 1 *Revelation 1:9-11.*
a) In what ways did John identify with his readers in verse 9?

b) Where was he when the Lord spoke to him?

c) What day was it?

d) How does he describe his inner feelings?

DAY 2 *Revelation 1:12-15.*
Close your eyes. Can you see what John saw?
a) What would it have reminded him of? (Mark 9:2,3)

b) Compare today's verses with Daniel 10:4-6. What do you think these descriptions tell us about the Lord Jesus?

DAY 3 *Revelation 1:17-20; Ezekiel 43:1-5*
a) What was John's reaction to seeing the glory of God in the face of Jesus Christ?

Jesus' description of Himself in verse 18 and His tenderness in raising up John, dramatises what Paul wrote in Romans 6:5-8.

b) What are we shown here?

QUESTIONS (contd.)

DAY 4   *Revelation 2:1, 8, 12.*
a) Which verses in chapter 1 do these verses repeat?

b) How do Revelation 2:7, 11, 17 and Romans 12:21 show that this book is relevant today?

c) If you are an 'overcomer', what promises are there for you?

DAY 5   *Revelation 2:1-7; Ephesians 1:15-17.*
a) For what was the church at Ephesus commended?

b) What does the risen Christ urge them to do?

DAY 6   *Revelation 2:8-11.*
a) What is meant by 'I know your ... poverty, yet you are rich!' and 'those who say they are Jews and are not'? (See Jas. 2:5 and Rom. 2:28, 29).

b) How would the description of Jesus in verse 8 strengthen the people for the suffering described in verse 10?

DAY 7   *Revelation 2:12-17: Numbers 25:1-3; 31:16.*
a) How do we know that persecution was already going on in this city?

b) What two sins, encouraged by Balaam thirteen centuries before, were being indulged in by some people in Pergamum?

NOTES

John was in exile on Patmos, an island in the Mediterranean, but as 'the curtain went up' that landscape faded, and he saw a totally different scene.

On the stage were seven lamps symbolising the seven churches, most likely the whole church. In the world, as the number seven in the Bible denotes completeness. Christians are those who shine like lights in the world. But this light is surpassed by the dazzling splendour of the one who identifies Himself as the resurrected Lord. He is the central figure, central to the church both then and now, and He holds His people (the stars) in His hand.

What an encouragement this is for us!

The Lord sees the church worldwide as one body, His body, and no one can pluck His people out of His hand.

But He has also given us a command:

'Let your light shine before men, that they may ... praise your Father in heaven' (Matt. 5:16).

Now the Lord has a special command for John:

'Write what you see and send it to the seven churches', that is, the church in the world.

The drama begins to unfold as the risen Christ dictates His letters to John.

EPHESUS

Some thirty years had passed since Paul had written to the Ephesians, commending them for their love and zeal. In the intervening time, the church had suffered but remained true to the faith.

But there is something lacking now.... LOVE. How about you? You may be a zealous upholder of sound doctrine, but are you filled with love – for the Lord, for your neighbours, for a fallen world?

The lampstand of Ephesus has indeed been removed over the years, and today no trace of the city remains.

SMYRNA

John, like Paul and Christ Himself knew the reality of persecution and suffering even to death.

Nowhere does the New Testament promise freedom from suffering in this life, but God does guarantee that though Christians may even suffer the death of the body, they will not suffer the death of the soul.

Would you be taken aback to find persecution knocking at your door tomorrow? What could you cling to? Paul said, 'I consider that our present sufferings are not worth comparing with the glory that is to be revealed in us' (Rom. 8:18).

PERGAMUM

In this city, Satan was working through the pressures of an influential, non-Christian society. Pergamum was not only the seat of government for the Roman imperial power with its emperor-worship, but also the centre for the worship of the Greek supreme god, 'Zeus the Saviour'. So the temptation to compromise or to give way under pressure was always present. The Christians needed to have a clear-cut distinction between right and wrong.

And don't we need that today too? It's important to know what rules God has laid down for us in His word, to call sin 'sin', and not to compromise just because 'everybody's doing it'.

'Let this message sink into the ears of anyone who listens' (LB).

This week adapt chapter 1:17 and 18 by saying to the Lord each day:

'I praise You because You are the First and the Last. You are the Living One, You were dead, and behold You are alive for ever and ever!'

STUDY 2

SCENE 1 (Continued)

QUESTIONS

DAY I *Revelation 2:18; 3:1, 7, 14.*
a) Look back to chapter 1 and find the descriptions of Christ which correspond to these verses.

b) Find the cities of the seven churches on a map of Bible days, if you can.

DAY 2 *Revelation 2:18-29; 1 Kings 16:31; 2 Kings 9:22.*
a) For what is the church at Thyatira commended?

b) What can you find out about the woman in that church who was of the same type as Jezebel?

DAY 3 *Revelation 3:1-6.*
a) What was wrong with the church in Sardis?

b) The Lord gave this church five pertinent commands. What were they?

DAY 4 *Revelation 3:7-13; Acts 14:27.*
The risen Lord has no fault to find with this church.
a) What is the 'open door' He has placed before them?

QUESTIONS (contd.)

b) Pick out a verse in today's reading which seems to you to be very important, and be ready to tell your group why.

DAY 5 *Revelation 3:14-22.*
a) What, in practical terms, do you think is meant by this church being lukewarm?

b) What hope is there for an individual belonging to this church?

DAY 6 *Revelation 2:7, 11, 17, 26, 28; 3:5, 12, 21.*
a) Make a list of the blessings in store for those who 'overcome' or 'win the victory'.

b) What does winning the victory mean for you personally?

DAY 7 *Revelation 7:14; 20:4, 6; 21:2, 27; 22:1, 2, 16.*
Beside yesterday's list of blessings, write the verse where these promises are echoed later in the book.

Read the notes on this study prayerfully and thoughtfully, giving yourself time to consider the questions.

NOTES

Remember we are looking at a stage where a drama is being enacted. In the centre stands the glorious Principal Actor in His pure robe and golden sash. Let us take to heart what He is saying, for it concerns us too. Let us hear what the Spirit is saying to us.

What is your church like?
* Faithful and full of good deeds, yet open to new theologies and idealisms, like Thyatira?
* A church which is dying without realising it – no one being converted, no spiritual growth, like Sardis?
* A church small in number, though with a missionary vision and zeal for obeying the Lord's commands, like Philadelphia?
* A lukewarm church, satisfied with things as they have always been, and knowing nothing of the new birth, like Laodicea?

Even if your church fits any of these descriptions, what about yourself?
* Are you like those in Thyatira who had not been led astray by false teaching? If so, hold on to the truths that you know, and stand firm.
* Are you like the few people in Sardis who had not soiled their clothes with sin? If so, keep yourself pure, dressed in Christ's righteousness, looking to the day when you will see him face to face.
* Are you like those in Philadelphia who kept their Lord's commands and endured patiently? If so, hold on to what you have, and remember you are a child of the King.
* Are you like the people in Laodicea who were complacent about going to heaven, without having the assurance the Bible gives? If so, open the door of your heart today to the living Christ, let Him come in and take control, and you will know the joy of close fellowship with Him.

* * *

So the curtain falls on the first scene of the drama. Chapter 1:12 tells us that John turned round and *saw* ... what we have been studying.

Now we say to ourselves, 'And what does he *see* next?' that will be Scene 2 which we will consider next week.

The words of Revelation 3:20 were written to those in the church. Learn them by heart and let their meaning sink deep into your soul as you consider the magnitude of Christ's offer to you.

'Here I am! I stand at the door and knock.
If anyone hears my voice and opens the door,
I will come in and eat with him, and he with me.'

Thank Him and praise Him for this wonderful promise.

STUDY 3

SCENE 2: A DOOR STANDING OPEN IN HEAVEN

QUESTIONS

DAY I *Revelation 4:1, 2: Ephesians 2:6, 7; 2 Corinthians 12:2-4; Acts 7:56*
a) What did John see and hear?

b) Do you think man will ever be able to penetrate into this heaven in a spacecraft? Why not?

DAY 2 *Revelation 4:2-6; Ezekiel 1:1-6, 26-28.*
a) What can you find in the Revelation verses that must have reminded John of Ezekiel's vision?

b) Who, in this scene, represents the whole church of God, before and after Christ? (See Rev. 21:12-14.)

DAY 3 *Revelation 4:3-6; Genesis 9:12-16; Exodus 19:16-19; Exodus 25:34-38; 2 Chronicles 4:2, 6.*
God used visual aids to teach His people in the days of Noah and Moses.
a) What do they tell us about God's character?

b) Why do you think He used concrete symbols?

DAY 4 *Revelation 4:6-11; Ezekiel 1:5-11; Romans 1:20.*
a) What qualities come to mind when you think of a lion, an ox, a man, an eagle?

QUESTIONS (contd.)

It is suggested that these living creatures represent everything that God has created – nature, which throbs with the ceaseless activity of God.

b) For what reason is God considered worthy of glory in Revelation 4:11?

DAY 5 *Revelation 5:1-5; Matthew 22:41-45; Isaiah 11:1, 10.*
a) Why did John weep bitterly?

b) Consider the two titles for Jesus given here. Can you explain them?

DAY 6 *Revelation 5:6-10; 1 Peter 1:18, 19.*
a) Where is Jesus, the Lamb of God, positioned in this scene?

b) Why was He deemed worthy to open the seals?

DAY 7 *Revelation 5:11-14*
Look back over chapters 4 and 5, and list the circles of worshippers John describes, from the throne outward. Our word 'worship' comes from 'worth-ship'. Try to imagine the worship in this scene, and then join the worshippers yourself in adoration before the throne.

NOTES

SCENE 1 was a vision of tremendous stillness, as the glorious risen Christ dictated His seven letters.

As the curtain rises on **SCENE 2**, our eyes are dazzled by the magnificent backdrop. As we become accustomed to the brightness, we see:

> God the Creator on His throne, the church of God, crown of creation, the world of nature, and the first symbols God used to teach man about Himself.

All creation joins in worshipping the creator God who is:

> supremely holy,
> all-powerful and mighty,
> eternal, everlasting.

What a sight!

But in all creation there is not found one single creature who is worthy to open the scroll, not one who could do anything about man's fallen state, or the curse on nature (Gen. 3:17).

And then the *Lamb* comes on the scene. He is the Lamb looking as if He had been slain, the Lamb of God who takes away the sin of the world, the Lamb with seven horns (complete power), and seven eyes (complete all-seeing wisdom), the Lamb who is worthy to receive power, wealth, wisdom and strength.

He takes the scroll from the hand of Him who sits on the throne, just as He took, at the beginning of His ministry here on earth, the scroll of the prophet Isaiah, in the synagogue at Nazareth. On that occasion, He explained that He was the fulfilment of God's plan for humanity, as foretold in the Old Testament.

Now He is seen again as the bridge between the old dispensation and the new, between those under the Law and those under Grace. Only in Christ crucified is to be found the answer to the riddle of life.

And a great new song bursts forth from God's people (elders) and God's world (living creatures). Nature joins the church in praising God, for He is not only Creator but also Redeemer. Redeemer, not only of man separated from God, but Redeemer of creation, which will one day be liberated from its bondage to decay (Rom. 8:21).

And as if that wasn't enough, we next see ten thousand times ten thousand angels encircling all those who are worshipping, adding their song of 'worthy is the Lamb'! Finally, the songs reach an unimaginable climax with every creature everywhere swelling the praise.

* * *

Which of these magnificent songs will you choose to use in your personal worship this week? That is your choice. Surely you are not going to miss out on adding your voice to the 'angels and archangels and all the company of heaven' as you come before His throne each day!

STUDY 4

SCENE 2 (Continued): SEVEN SEALS OPENED

QUESTIONS

DAY 1   *Revelation 6:1-4; Matthew 24:3-8.*
The same Jesus (the Lamb) who opens the seals, is the one who told His disciples what the future would hold.
a) Sum up in one word each, what the first and second seals predicted.

b) Did Jesus say these things would happen from the time He was speaking, onwards, or not until the end of the age?

DAY 2   *Revelation 6:5-8.*
a) What word in Matthew 24:7 describes what the black horse and its rider showed?

Think of some areas in the world which are experiencing this today.

b) The fourth seal: remembering that we are being shown events which will occur right down the centuries, what things will kill a sizeable number of people?

DAY 3   *Revelation 6:9-11; Matthew 24:9-14.*
a) Why were the martyrs told to wait a little longer for justice?

b) What did Jesus say would be the sign of 'the end'?

(*Note*: 'inhabitants of the earth', 6:10, are those who are not 'citizens of heaven', Phil. 3:20.)

DAY 4   *Revelation 6:12-17; Matthew 24:29-31* (vv. 15-28 refer to the fall of Jerusalem in AD 70).
a) Make a list of events common to both these passages.

QUESTIONS (contd.)

b) What are they describing?

c) Does all this frighten you?

DAY 5 *Revelation 7:1-3; Ezekiel 9:3-6; Ephesians 1:13, 14*
a) What does the symbolism of the mark, or seal, signify?

b) When is the Christian 'sealed'?

c) What does this guarantee?

DAY 6 *Revelation 7:4-10; Romans 2:28, 29; Galatians 6:16.*
a) What did John *hear*? Think of verses 4-8 as a diagram of the Israel of God, and the number 144,000 as symbolic of all believers from Old Testament times to the Lord's return.

b) What did John *see*? How many were there?

DAY 7 *Revelation 7:11–8:1.*
a) Find two reasons why these people are entitled to stand before the throne.

b) What promises are there in verses 15-17 for Christians?

c) What happened when the seventh seal was opened?

NOTES

The action in the drama speeds up. See the four horses with their riders flash across as the **first four seals** are opened. They are portraying events that will continue to occur, right through history.

Hear the cry of the four living creatures who represent the world of nature. What do they shout each time?

'Come!'

Why do they call 'Come'? They are not calling John, for he has already come to the vantage point from which he is surveying the whole scene. Surely they are not calling the riders, inviting conquest, strife, scarcity and death to ruin the world which they represent In any case, only the second horse is said to have 'come out'.

The Greek word used for 'come' in this case is the one used in Revelation 1:7, 'Look, he is coming', and in 22:20, 'Yes, I am coming soon'. (A different Greek word is used in Rev. 17:1 and 21:9.)

From Romans 8:19-22 we know that the whole creation yearns for the coming of Christ to deliver it from its bondage of decay. In the same way, the martyrs that are seen when the **fifth seal** is opened, cry out 'How long?' that is, 'How long till you come again?'

* * *

So we see the Lamb opening the **sixth seal.** And at last we have a reference point in time. The vivid events here herald the final coming of our Lord.

'The great day of their wrath has come' (6:1 7). 'They will see the Son of Man coming on the clouds of the sky, with power and great glory' (Matt. 24:30). That day will spell the end of the entire universe as we know it.

Evil and suffering have been and will be rampant from the time of John's vision till the day of Jesus' return. Christians will not be exempt. Many will suffer and even die for their faith. BUT ... their eternal destiny is secure. Their eternal safety is never in question.

Remember the glorious unfolding vision of chapters 4 and 5?

* God is still on the throne.
* Christ is at the centre.
* It is He who is finally in control.
* All power is given to Him in heaven and earth.

Like John, we need a clear and unshaken picture of where the real power lies. Only then can we view events on earth in their true perspective.

Chapter 7: 'After this, I saw...' writes John. As the Lord has shown him in six seals the pageant of woes and suffering right up to the end of time, and then His second coming, there can be nothing chronologically 'after this'.

So what is now shown to him is a new view of the same thing, but from God's point of view. God's control ensures that His church is sealed and secure *before* the horsemen of chapter 6 ride forth and the land is harmed (7:3).

* * *

Scene 2 of this heavenly drama certainly has an exciting cast:

the angels, elders and living creatures of chapters 4 and 5, the horsemen of chapter 6, the four wind-angels, chapter 7, the innumerable 144,000 in their white robes.

At the climax we see them all praising and glorifying God for ever and ever!

* * *

So what about the seventh seal? Why half an hour's interval between Scenes 2 and 3?

Seals I to 6 have taken us through history, showing what will be the experience of the church during that time, up till the end of the world. When Seal Seven is actually broken open, there is silence. God has nothing to say at this point There is another world to come, but John must be given time to meditate on what he has seen concerning world events, the eternal security of believers, and the assurance that God is still on the throne.

* * *

As you worship the Lord in your own Quiet Time this week, use the words of Revelation 7:12. Think about each word as you say it.

STUDY 5

SCENE 3: SEVEN TRUMPETS SOUNDED

QUESTIONS

DAY 1 *Revelation 8:2-6; 6:9, 10; Exodus 3:7; 30:7, 8.*
a) In what way was the cry, or prayer, of the saints similar to that of God's people in Egypt?

b) Discuss why incense is used to symbolise prayer. (See Rev. 5:8.) Use these thoughts to help you when you pray.

DAY 2 *Revelation 8:7-12: Exodus 7:17-19; 9:22-26; 10:21-23.*
Compare the devastation of the first four trumpets with the plagues of Egypt.
a) Is John shown here that destruction will be total or partial?

b) In the light of Revelation 9:20, 21, how should we view major catastrophes in our world today?

DAY 3 *Revelation 8:13–9:12; Exodus 10:12-15; Matthew 11:21-24; Luke 10:18.*
We need to see the biblical symbolism in this passage.
a) Who is the one who unleashes these terrifying hordes?

b) Where do they come from?

c) Whom do they torment?

d) Why does the Lord Jesus proclaim woes on the towns of Galilee?

DAY 4 *Revelation 9:13-21.*
a) Compare verse 15 with verse 5. What was the difference between these demonic horsemen and the locusts?

QUESTIONS (contd.)

b) Did the unbelievers repent when they saw the others being killed?

c) What might they have learned about God from these events?

d) Is there a parallel today?

DAY 5 *Revelation 10:1-11; Ephesians 3:4-6; Ezekiel 2:9–3:4.*
a) What is meant by 'the mystery of God' (v. 7)?

b) What two things was John told he must do?

c) Why would that be a bitter experience?

DAY 6 *Revelation 11:1-14; Zechariah 4:2-6.*
a) The two witnesses symbolize the church in the world.

b) What can you find out about them?

c) While the church maintains her witness, the unbelievers seem to dominate the world. Which verses bring this out?

DAY 7 *Revelation 11:15-18.*
a) To what period do these verses refer?

Compare the description of God in verse 17 with that in 1:4-8.
b) What do you find?

c) Why are the unbelieving nations angry?

NOTES

The curtain rises.

'I saw the seven angels who stand before God,' writes John, 'and to them were given seven trumpets.'

Can you imagine the scene? How glorious! What will these seven angelic heralds proclaim?

As the drama unfolds with terrifying action, we can discern the purpose behind the trumpet calls. God is not willing that any should perish, but that all should come to repentance, so He uses drastic methods to make unbelievers acknowledge Him, and to offer them mercy while there is still time.

Perhaps we need to remind ourselves that the book of Revelation was not written like history, in chronological order.

SCENE 2 (breaking open the seals) shows what is happening throughout history, up to the return of Christ with particular reference to what the church will have to suffer.

SCENE 3 (sounding the trumpets) deals with the same time span, but proclaims a series of warnings to the *unbelieving world.*

These two scenes run parallel in time. They may be looked at as two sides of the same coin.

THE FIRST TRUMPET: hail affects one third of man's environment.
THE SECOND TRUMPET: a mountain destroys one third of the sea and shipping.
THE THIRD TRUMPET: a star poisons drinking water (natural resources).
THE FOURTH TRUMPET: the light by which man sees is affected.

Certain disasters throughout history may come to mind as we read this section. This is not surprising, as the vision portrays aspects of the world situation which may be true at any time. God means these events to serve as a warning to unbelievers, who need to admit that God is at work, and turn to Him.

THE FIFTH TRUMPET: unbelievers themselves are affected. Perhaps things like drugs, disease resulting from sin, crime, etc. can come into this category.
THE SIXTH TRUMPET: this brings death, and is the final warning to those who

are left alive. The Lord sometimes uses the death of a loved one to bring a person to Himself.

When the SEVENTH TRUMPET is sounded, it is **too late**. Surely these are the saddest words that can be uttered: 'too late'.

Have you a friend or loved one who has not yet come to Christ?
Then pray urgently, and witness in whatever way the Lord leads you, as one day it will be TOO LATE.

* * *

Many interpretations have been given of Revelation 11:1-14. The thoughts suggested in the study are described in detail in Michael Wilcock's book *The Message of Revelation*. The symbolism may be confusing to us, but let's remember that while the gospel is still being preached we know we are living in the 42 months (1,260 days) period.

As the curtain comes down on Scene 3, our eyes once again focus on the throne, and the redeemed singing praises to the Lord God Almighty, for history is past and

> 'the kingdom of the world has become
> the kingdom of our Lord and of His Christ,
> and He will reign for ever and ever!'

* * *

See if you can find some music set to the words of 11:15 or 17, and play it in your Quiet Time. It might be the Hallelujah Chorus from Handel's Messiah, or 'We give thanks, Lord God Almighty' from Scripture in Song Vol. 2 (Songs of the Kingdom).

STUDY 6

SCENE 4: SEVEN VISIONS OF COSMIC CONFLICT

QUESTIONS

DAY 1   *Revelation 11:19–12:6; Genesis 37:9-11; Romans 9:5.*
The characters introduced.
a) Can you discover who the woman represents?

b) Who is the child? (Ps. 2:7-9)

c) And the dragon? (Rev. 11:9)

DAY 2   *Revelation 12:7–13:1; Ephesians 6:12.*
The plot, spanning history.
Read verses 9 and 10 carefully, and compare them with Matthew 12:28; 28:18; and Luke 10:17, 18.
a) When does this suggest that Satan's defeat came? (1 John 3:8)

b) How can Christians overcome the devil?

DAY 3   *Revelation 13:2-10; Daniel 7:2-7, 15-17.*
The beast from the sea.
a) What did the dragon give the beast?

b) So what does this beast symbolize, appearing as he does during the gospel age of 42 months?

QUESTIONS (contd.)

DAY 4   *Revelation 13:11-18; Matthew 24:10-13; 1 John 4:1-3.*
The beast from the earth.
a) What can you find in this passage to show that this beast stands for false religion, or any perversion of Christianity?

b) Can you think of any examples of this in history?

DAY 5   *Revelation 14:1-13; 2 Timothy 2:19.*
a) Remembering the symbolism, what can you find out about the redeemed (i.e. the whole church) from verses 1-5?

b) What three messages did the three angels proclaim? (vv. 6-11)

DAY 6   *Revelation 14:14-20; Matthew 13:27-30, 37-42.*
a) What does this passage describe?

b) Do you know for certain which group you will be in?

c) On what do you base your assurance?

DAY 7   *Revelation 15:14; Exodus 15:1, 2; Romans 6:22; Colossians 1:13, 14.*
a) Why are the song of Moses and the song of the Lamb the same thing?

b) What aspects of God's character does the song praise?

NOTES

How awe-inspiring is the opening of Scene 4! God is in His holy temple. The thunder and lightning associated with His presence in the Old Testament bear witness to this.

Look, there is the ark, symbol of His covenant, His agreement to rescue people from their enemies. At the end of this scene we shall hear the redeemed singing the song of Moses and the Lamb, for God has kept His covenant, His promise, and has rescued them from the great enemy, Satan.

This scene shows us world history from yet another angle: the constant spiritual battle between God and Satan. The characters in this part of the drama are:

THE WOMAN   First identified as the nation of Israel, the human stock from which Christ came, and later, after Christ's ascension, as the new Israel, the church. Notice that God protects her for the period of the gospel age, 42 months (1,260 days).

THE CHILD   Our Lord Jesus Christ is glimpsed at His incarnation and then at His ascension. His incarnation was the point at which He first came within the devil's grasp, His ascension the point at which He escaped from it forever.

THE DRAGON   Satan appears with seven heads (authority), ten horns (strength) and seven crowns (prince of this world).

Next in rapid succession come seven visions, seven pictures of which John wrote:

'and I saw' (13:1), 'then I saw' (13:11), 'then I looked' (14:1), Then I saw' (14:6), 'I looked' (14:14), 'I saw' (15:1), 'and I saw' (15:2).

1. **The beast from the sea.** This vision would have brought to John's mind the Roman empire, the great political power of his day, but succeeding generations of Christians have found equivalents of it also in their day. Throughout the church age this beast will be active, bringing conflict to God's people by the power and authority of the state.

2. **The beast from the earth.** How cleverly Satan counterfeits true Christianity, with his veneer of religion, concern with worship, and appeal to the magical!

How should we interpret 'the number of the beast' (13:8)? Michael Wilcock, in the book we are following, writes:

'Let us paraphrase the verse, as it might have been read to those original hearers. "Let him who has understanding work out a number for the beast, a human number, a code such as we have symbolizing the church (144,000) and the church age (42 months). What might we suggest? A number as close as may be to perfection, but not achieving it." And because the beast in all its activities is persistently missing the mark, the number John writes here is not just six (one short of seven, the symbol of perfection) but 666.'

Note that the AV, RSV and NW have the correct translation, 'calculate, or reckon, the *number*', it is not, as in GNB and LB, 'figure out the *meaning* of the number'. We know the meaning, 666 stands for the beast from the earth.

3. **The Lamb and His followers.** It is refreshing to gaze on this vision, in marked contrast to what has gone before.
4. **The angel messengers.**
5. **The final reaping.**
6. **A short preview of Scene 5.**
7. **The song of victory.**

* * *

Use the words of the song in Revelation 15:3, 4 each day this week, as you come before the Lord in worship. Say the words aloud, and see what effect they have on you by the end of the week.

STUDY 7
SCENE 5: SEVEN BOWLS POURED OUT

QUESTIONS

DAY 1 *Revelation 15;1, 5-8; Exodus 40:1-3, 34, 35; Leviticus 16:24; Numbers 1:51, 53.*
a) In the days of Moses, what impression would the people have had of God?

b) How is that impression conveyed in these verses in Revelation?

DAY 2 *Revelation 15:5-8; Isaiah 33:14; Luke 12:4, 5; Hebrews 10:31.*
a) Do we sometimes overlook this side of God's character?

b) Jesus said we should fear God. Why?

c) In connection with God's wrath, why is it significant that He lives for ever and ever (v. 7)?

DAY 3 *Revelation 16:1-3; I Samuel 5:1, 6-12; 6:1-11, 19, 20.*
a) What happened at the end of the incident reported in I Samuel, that does not happen when the *First Bowl* is poured out?

b) What two other places in the Bible mention something like the plague of the *Second Bowl?*

DAY 4 *Revelation 16:4-7; 6:9, 10.*
a) Why was the *Third Bowl* of God's wrath seen to be a just punishment?

QUESTIONS (contd.)

b) What is meant by 'the altar' responding (v. 7)?

DAY 5 *Revelation 16:8-11; 8:7–9:6.*
a) How is the sequence of bowls (punishments) different from the sequence of trumpets (warnings)?

b) As the *Fourth* and *Fifth Bowls* were poured out, what did the people do?

c) And what did they refuse to do?

DAY 6 *Revelation 16:12-16; Matthew 24:42-44; 1 Thessalonians 5:1, 2; 2 Peter 3:10-13.*
a) How were the kings of the world persuaded to gather for battle at Armageddon?

b) What reassurance is there for Christians in these passages?

c) What should our attitude be when thinking about this final battle?

DAY 7 *Revelation 16:17-21; John 19:30; Hebrews 12:25-29*
a) To what was the loud voice from the throne referring?

b) And to what was Jesus referring on the cross?

c) When the heavens and the earth pass away, what can Christians be thankful for?

NOTES

As the curtain falls on Scene 4, perhaps we should break for the interval, because it will give us time to think back over what we have seen.

Scene 1   opened up the condition of the church in the world.

Scene 2   the seals were broken open, to reveal troubles that would affect the church and world alike, with one quarter of the earth destroyed.

Scene 3   the trumpets proclaimed open-ended warnings, offering men a choice of repentance or doom. A third of the earth was destroyed as a divine warning.

Scene 4   opened out for us the spiritual conflict of history.

But as we return and take our seats for the second half of the performance, we shall find that, increasingly, there is a feeling of 'closing in'. God's wrath is completed (15:1), the whole of unrepentant humanity ends in disaster (Scene 5), anti-God world power is totally overthrown (Scene 6), and Satan himself is destroyed (Scene 7).

In these scenes there are no longer warnings, but punishments, not openings, but closings, not beginnings, but endings.

* * *

We have tackled some big issues in this study:

the holiness of God, the wrath of God, eternal punishment, His judgment on those who refuse to obey Him as Lord, the second coming of Christ, the final battle, the end of the heavens and the earth as we know them.

Will the world really come to an end? Will the things we have read about really happen?

If you acknowledge that the words of Jesus are true, and believe the Bible to be the inspired word of God, then you can be in no doubt that the answer is 'yes'.

Some people say: 'I don't think God would punish people like that', or 'I think we'll all be together in heaven when we die', but it is not what we *think* that matters.

Remember what Jesus said: 'Heaven and earth will pass away, but my words will never pass away' (Mark 13:31).

* * *

Worship God this week with the thoughts expressed in Revelation 16:7,

'Yes, Lord God Almighty, true and just are your judgments',

and work through what they mean for you.

STUDY 8
SCENE 6: SEVEN WORDS OF JUSTICE

QUESTIONS

DAY 1   *Revelation 17:1-6a; 13:11, 12; Jeremiah 3:1, 6-9.*
The sin of Babylon.
a) In what sense has Babylon (godless civilization) committed adultery?

b) In what ways are we shown that Babylon is influential (17:2), evil (v. 3), attractive (v. 4) yet repulsive (v. 6)?

c) Do you agree that the non-Christian world can be all of these things?

DAY 2   *Revelation 17:6b-18; Judges 11:9-11; Ezekiel 26:7.*
The mystery of Babylon.
a) Taken collectively, what kind of being do the seven heads, hills and kings of the godless world power suggest?

b) How is the Lamb described?

c) How are we shown that God is supreme and in control? (Compare v. 17 with Acts 4:27, 28.)

DAY 3   *Revelation 18:1-3; 14:8; Daniel 5:22-31.*
The fall of Babylon.
a) How does the historical fall of Babylon give us a picture of the doom awaiting Satan's world empire?

b) Can you find out reasons for the fall of some of the empires of the past, e.g. Persia, Greece, Rome, the Third Reich?

QUESTIONS (contd.)

DAY 4 *Revelation 18:4-20; Jeremiah 51:44-48; 2 Corinthians 6:14-17.*
The judgment of Babylon.
a) What two things are God's people told to do in these verses?

b) What three groups of people mourn over the fallen world power?

DAY 5 *Revelation 18:21-24; Jeremiah 51:59-64; Matthew 23:29-37.*
The destruction of Babylon.
a) How does this passage indicate that the destruction of the city will be total and for ever?

b) Which city does Jesus condemn as murderer of the prophets?

DAY 6 *Revelation 19:1-5; 6:10; 16:5-7.*
The doom song of Babylon.
a) Do you know what the word 'hallelujah' means?

b) What causes the great multitude to praise God at this point?

c) How does the voice from the throne describe those who are worthy to praise God? (See also 19:10.)

DAY 7 *Revelation 19:6-10; Philippians 2:12, 13.*
The successor of Babylon.
a) In what ways is the Bride in contrast to the great prostitute?

b) How does the Philippians reading explain the fact that she made the dress herself, yet it was given to her to wear?

NOTES

What a colourful and exotic scene is before our eyes as the curtain rises this time!

Look at the central figure. The woman, seated on a scarlet beast, is dressed in purple and scarlet, glittering with gold, precious stones and pearls, and she drinks from a golden cup. See the kings of the earth arrayed in front of her, infatuated by her beauty. The woman is certainly attractive – after all, don't many of our TV shows and movies today revolve around unfaithfulness and adultery? The godless world still tempts people away from God.

But the climax of the drama of this scene comes when doom is pronounced, and Babylon the Great falls. Now the kings of the earth, terrified, huddle together in one corner of the stage, and weep and mourn over her. The merchants appear next, devastated because they have lost their trade. We see a glittering array of merchandise, from gold and silver to ivory and marble, from myrrh and frankincense to horses and carriages. Then the sea captains and sailors take their place on stage, bemoaning the fact that all their income has been derived from the city which now lies in ruins. What a scene!

Gradually the noise of weeping subsides, and a mighty angel picks up a boulder and hurls it into the sea. There is deathly silence. No music, no daily work, no happy occasions such as weddings. Nothing.

Babylon is gone.

And then ... the roar of a great multitude in heaven shouting, HALLELUJAH!

What a song of praise erupts from the whole company of heaven, like the roar of rushing waters or peals of thunder!

'Hallelujah! For the Lord God Omnipotent reigneth!'

Can you wonder that Handel, the 18th Century composer, was so moved by this scene that he wrote the inspired Hallelujah Chorus, which triumphantly closes Part Two of the Messiah? Listen to his own words, as the music flowed from his mind:

'I did think I did see all Heaven before me, and the great God Himself.'

This is just what John saw too, in this scene. May the Lord grant each one of us a vision of His glory, His majesty and His power, so that we too may rejoice and be glad, knowing for sure that the Lord God Almighty reigns, and He will reign for ever and ever.

As the curtain falls, we catch a glimpse of that pure and lovely figure, the Bride of Christ, arrayed in her perfect wedding dress. We long to have a good look at her, to enjoy her beauty, but we must wait a little longer for that.

Have you been moved by the events of this scene? Five tremendous 'words of justice' have described the pomp and power of Satan's activity in the world. But the Babylon they set before us is a city doomed to perish. The smoking ruins of that city disappear as the host of heavenly spectators come into view, and the scene culminates in the celebration of the triumph of God over Satan.

No wonder John was overcome with awe, and fell at the feet of the angel who revealed all this to him. Although it was misplaced worship, yet it shows the effect the scene had on him. What effect has it had on you?

* * *

Choose your own verses for your personal worship this week.

STUDY 9

SCENE 7: SEVEN VISIONS OF ULTIMATE REALITY
(each introduced by the words 'I saw ...')

QUESTIONS

DAY 1 *Revelation 19:11-16; 1:16; 3:14; John 1:1; Psalm 2:9; Isaiah 63:1-3.*
a) Who is the rider on the white horse? What names is He given?

b) Is there any time referred to in this passage, or can we understand that the conquering King is leading His army out even today, to fight against evil? (Eph. 6:10-12)

DAY 2 *Revelation 19:17, 18; Ezekiel 39:17-20.*
a) How do these passages show that there is no doubt about the outcome of the battle?

b) What contrasting invitation is given in Matthew 22:14?

DAY 3 *Revelation 19:19-21; Matthew 13:40-42.*
We have met the beast and the false prophet before.
a) What were they called? (Rev. 13:1, 2, 11, 12; 17:3.)

b) What do they symbolize?

c) When does Jesus tell us these things will be?

DAY 4 *Revelation 20:1-3; Luke 11:20-22; Matthew 12:29.*
a) How do Jesus' words about the strong man being bound relate to this passage, assuming that the 1,000 years (like the 144,000) is a symbolic number?

QUESTIONS (contd.)

b) Galatians 3:14. How does this verse show that Satan had the nations (Gentiles) altogether in his power until the coming of Christ?

c) Can you see how the gospel age may be represented by the 1,000 years?

DAY 5   *Revelation 20:4-6; John 5:24; Ephesians 2:4-6.*
a) What do these verses suggest the first resurrection is? Revelation 20:7-10; 2 Thessalonians 2:1-8.

b) Find verses in previous chapters which refer to this final battle.

DAY 6   *Revelation 20:11-15; 2 Corinthians 5:10; Hebrews 9:27.*
a) How will the dead be judged?

b) By whose righteousness will Christians be judged (Phil. 3:9)?

c) And where are their names written?

d) What is the Christian's response to those who believe in reincarnation?

DAY 7   *Revelation 21:1-8; Isaiah 65:17-19; 2 Peter 3:13; John 4:14.*
a) What blessings are promised here for those who live with God in eternity?

b) What significance is there in the names God gives Himself?

NOTES

As Scene 7 begins, we can hardly take in everything that is happening. Our tidy minds would like to fit in events in order, and see what is going to happen when. But God's ways are perfect, and this is what we are shown:

The King of Kings and Lord of Lords rides forth, followed by His armies,
the angel summons the birds to a feast of carrion,
the beast and the false prophet are thrown into the lake of fire,
the devil is bound and thrown into the pit,
the redeemed reign with Christ,
Satan has a last fling and is then thrown into the lake of fire,
and the One on the great white throne judges all mankind.

And then, after all the turmoil, comes peace as we see the new heaven, the new earth, and the Holy City, the Bride of Christ.

Can you imagine John trying to take everything in, to write down what he saw? Turning to look at first one and then another, he writes, 'I saw a white horse ... I saw an angel ... I saw the beast ... I saw thrones ... I saw a great white throne ... then I saw a new heaven and a new earth.' It may be mind-boggling to us, but how much more to John, as the vivid scenes flashed before his eyes in all their originality.

Have you noticed how each scene, from Scene 2 onwards, has finished with a picture of the eternal destiny of believers? As we watch the closing moments of Scene 7, we shall see that it, too, ends with the reality of eternity. 'Here comes the Bride', but look, she is a city, the place where God will dwell with men! And we have a foretaste of what is to come in Scene 8, as we are briefly shown:

God's city	21:2
God's dwelling	21:3
God's world renewed	21:4, 5a
God's word validated	21:5b
God's work completed	21:6a
God's final blessing	21:6b, 7
and God's final curse	21:8

Find some ideas for your praise and worship times this week from Revelation 21:3-7.

STUDY 10

QUESTIONS

DAY 1   **1. God's city.** *Revelation 21:9-11; Matthew 16:18; 1 Corinthians 3:9; Ephesians 5:25-27.*
a) What are the bride and the city both pictures of?

b) In what ways is God preparing us (21:2) for that day?

c) What is one characteristic of the city?

DAY 2   **God's city (cont.).** *Revelation 21:12-21; Ephesians 2:19-22; Isaiah 61:10.*
a) How are we shown that the city is made up of all God's people down through the ages?

b) How do we know that every individual is known to God?

c) How is the beauty of the city described in Revelation? In Isaiah?

DAY 3   **2. God's dwelling.** *Revelation 21:2, 3, 22-27; Isaiah 60:3, 11, 18, 19.*
a) Why is there no temple in the city?

b) Why no sun or moon?

c) How do we know it is a *holy* city?

QUESTIONS (contd.)

DAY 4 **3. God's world renewed.** *Revelation 22:1-5; 21:4, 5a; Genesis 2:8-10; 3:17; Ezekiel 47:12.*
a) What difference can you find between the garden in Genesis and that in Revelation?

DAY 5 **4. God's word validated.** *Revelation 22:6-10; 21:6a; Hebrews 1:1, 2; 2 Timothy 3:16.*
a) How is God described here?

b) Why is Jesus called 'the Word' in John 1:1, 2?

DAY 6 **5. God's work completed.** *Revelation 22:11-15; 21:6a; 7:14.*
a) What can you find in these verses to show that there is no 'second chance' to accept salvation after death?

b) On what grounds are the blessed accepted?

c) Do you expect to go to heaven? Why?

DAY 7 **6. God's final blessing.** *Revelation 22:16, 17; 21:6b, 7.*
a) What is the free gift that is offered?

b) Have you taken it?

7. God's final curse. *Revelation 22:18, 19; 21:8.*
c) What is the warning to anyone who alters the gospel to suit himself, or tries to disprove biblical doctrine?

SAY THE WORDS OF VERSES 20 and 21 TOGETHER AS A GROUP.

NOTES

As the climax to the drama we see a scene of breathtaking beauty. The holy bride, the holy city, comes down from God. The glory, the brilliance, the magnificence of it all is unlike anything we have ever seen before.

And then suddenly we realise ... we are part of it. For the holy city is the church – what she will be when Christ presents her to Himself without stain or wrinkle or any other blemish. She will be holy and blameless. And right now He is preparing her for that day:

* He has given us His Spirit who lives within us,
* Our eternal future is secure with all the saints (Luke 13:28, 29),
* He knows each one of us and has a plan for our lives,
* He has made us beautiful with His righteousness.

Should we not live every day with a sense of our high calling in Christ, our hearts and minds set on things above?

Then we turn and see, as John saw, not only a city but a garden.

Paradise regained. And we are there too. We serve and worship Him, His name is written on our foreheads, we reign for ever and ever.

So the great drama ends, and John testifies to the truth of what he has written. But it is not John, but Jesus, who has the final word. He has a relevant message for each one of us.

'Behold, I am coming soon' (22:7, 12).
'Yes, I am coming soon' (22:20).

Can you sense the urgency?

'I am the bright Morning Star'.

He heralds the dawn of eternity, telling us that this life is only a prelude to the real life of the world to come.

When will He come? We don't know.

Are you ready if He should come today?
Can you honestly say with John, 'Come, Lord Jesus'?

Worship God this week with any of the wonderful verses you have used throughout this study, and thank Him for what He has shown you in the past ten weeks.

ANSWER GUIDE

The following pages contain an Answer Guide. It is recommended that answers to the questions be attempted before turning to this guide. It is only a guide and the answers given should not be treated as exhaustive.

GUIDE TO INTRODUCTORY STUDY

Do make sure you have a copy of *The Message of Revelation* as mentioned at the beginning of the study.

It is most important to help your group understand that from Scene 2 (Study 4) to Scene 7 (Study 9) we are given an overall view of history from John's day to eternity, **in each scene**. Thus the scenes are concurrent rather than consecutive. Michael Wilcock brings this out clearly in his book

Scene 2: **Seals.** The world will suffer conquest and scarcity, strife and death, and even the church will not be exempt BUT punishment will come on Satan's kingdom, while the redeemed are assured of eternal safety.

Scene 3: **Trumpets.** To warn mankind, God touches the environment, commerce, resources and vision, sends personal troubles and death. BUT at trumpet 7 the kingdoms of the world have become the kingdom of our Lord.

Scene 4: **Visions.** Great spiritual forces are engaged in the cosmic struggle of history. BUT God holds the trump card at the harvest time, after which the redeemed stand victorious over the beast

Scene 5: **Bowls.** God punishes unrepentant man by land and sea, water and fire. BUT He will do more than this. The whole evil society is thrown into disarray, the final battle is fought and time and history are replaced by eternity.

Scene 6: **Words.** We have a picture of Satan's evil activity in the world throughout time. BUT his great empire is doomed, destroyed, and the Lamb and His bride prepare for the wedding feast.

Scene 7: **Visions.** The whole drama of sin and redemption is described in the most basic terms, with emphasis on the final destruction of evil, the judgment, the new heaven and the new earth.

* * *

We realise that some commentators and perhaps some people in your group hold different views from those expressed in the book *The Message of Revelation* but we feel this interpretation has much to commend it. Michael Wilcock gives a clear, logical presentation, using Scripture to interpret Scripture, and if any problems arise in your discussions, we suggest you refer people to the full explanations given in his book

The study of Revelation is an important one. It crystallizes Christian beliefs about God, creation, mankind, sin and eternal destiny, which are vital for us to have firmly established in our minds today. We shall see how God's truth revealed in His word is the exact opposite to some increasingly popular views which are propagated by the New Age Movement.

GOD'S TRUTH		NEW AGE VIEWS
		'Life force' is an impersonal force.
God is a personal being who sits		It is energy and ultimate reality, but has no
on the throne.	4:2	qualifies or attributes.
He is holy, almighty, and He is		All of creation is God. Creation is sacred
Lord.	4:8	and divine. Humanity is not distinct from
He is the object of worship	4:10	God; all is one (monism).
and the creator of all things.	4:11	
Sin is real and evokes the wrath		There are no absolutes, no right or wrong.
of God.	19:2	Therefore our problem is not sin but
Man can only be cleansed from		ignorance, so our real need is for
sin by faith in Christ's atoning		enlightenment.
death.	5:9	
		After we die, we are reincarnated, and come
Man dies physically only once,		back to earth in another form. Reincarnation
and judgment follows.	6:9, 10	is an upward evolution both at the personal
	20:11-13	level and for the human race as a whole.

GUIDE TO STUDY 1

DAY 1 a) As brother, one who shared their suffering, their patient endurance, and the kingdom of God.
b) On the island of Patmos.
c) The Lord's day.
d) In the Spirit.

DAY 2 a) The transfiguration.
b) Suggestions: Linen, purity; gold, kingship; white hair, wisdom; eyes, penetrating vision; feet, strength; voice, beauty.

DAY 3 a) He fell at His feet as though dead.
b) That we must come to a place where we die to self, so that He can raise us up to become new creations (Eph. 2:4-6).

DAY 4 a) Verses 12, 13, 16, 17 and 18.
b) Present tense: The Spirit 'says' or 'is saying'.
c) Tree of life, safety from the second death, hidden manna, new name.

DAY 5 a) Hard work, perseverance, faithfulness, resistance to false teaching.
b) Remember the love they used to have, and repent.

DAY 6 a) They were financially poor, but spiritually rich. They were descendants of Abraham but were not the true Israel.
b) Even though they should die the martyr's death, they will be resurrected as Christ was.

DAY 7 a) One faithful witness, Antipas, had been put to death.
b) Eating food offered to idols, and sexual immorality.

GUIDE TO STUDY 2

DAY 1 a) 1:14, 15; 1:16; 1:18; 1:5.
b) *Leaders*, bring a map with the places clearly marked.

DAY 2 a) Love, faith, service, perseverance and constant improvement.
b) She called herself a prophetess; her false teaching led others into immorality and eating food offered to idols; she refused to repent; she taught about Satan.

DAY 3 a) It was dead and didn't know it.
b) Wake up; strengthen what remains; remember what you have heard; obey it; repent.

DAY 4 a) The door of faith into the kingdom of God.
b) Personal.

DAY 5 a) Apathetic, not on fire for the Lord but professing to be Christians, nominal Christianity.
b) The Lord still loves each one (3:19) but repentance is the only way to be forgiven.

DAY 6 a) 1) The right to eat from the tree of life.
2) Not being harmed by the second death.
3) Hidden manna and the white stone.
4) Authority over the nations, morning star.
5) White robes, names in the book of Life.
6) A pillar in the new Jerusalem.
7) The right to sit with Christ on His throne.
b) Personal.

DAY 7 a) 22:1, 2
b) 20:6
c) -
d) 20:4, 22:16
e) 7:14, 21:27
f) 21:2
g) 20:4

· · · · ·

49

GUIDE TO STUDY 3

DAY 1 a) A door open in heaven. A voice inviting him to come in.
b) No. It is the place where God, who is Spirit, dwells.

DAY 2 a) Storms, lightning, living creatures, a throne, a rainbow.
b) The twenty-four elders (twelve tribes of Israel, O.T., and twelve apostles, N.T.)

DAY 3 a) He is merciful, awesome, majestic and powerful, pure, glorious, and the light of the world.
b) They were things people could easily understand.

DAY 4 a) Majesty, strength, wisdom, loftiness.
b) Because He is the creator.

DAY 5 a) Because no one could be found who was worthy to open the scroll.
b) 'The Lion of the tribe of Judah.' The lion is king of the beasts; Judah is the tribe from which the first and greatest kings came. 'The Root of David (Jesse).' The creator of man from whom David came, also the branch from His ancestor David.

DAY 6 a) In the centre of (or in front of) the throne.
b) Because He has paid for man's salvation with His blood.

DAY 7 Living creatures, elders, thousands of angels, every creature. If you can, bring to your group a tape of 'Worthy is the Lamb' from the 'Messiah', to play at the end.

GUIDE TO STUDY 4

DAY 1   a) First seal: conquest. Second seal: war, strife.
b) From that time onwards (Matt. 24:6).

DAY 2   a) Famine. The Revelation passage shows scarcity of food.
b) War, famine, disease, wild beasts (carnage on the roads?)

DAY 3   a) Because there would be more who would die for their faith.
b) When the gospel has been preached to all people.

DAY 4   a) Earthquake; sun, moon and stars affected; nations fearful.
b) The day when Jesus will return.
c) Personal.
(*Leader*: This could be an opportunity to help those who are not sure of their salvation; 2 Pet. 3:10-13 for Christians.)

DAY 5   a) It signifies that the people belong to God, and He protects them.
b) When he believes, that is, is converted.
c) It guarantees our inheritance: eternity with God.

DAY 6   a) He heard the symbolic number of those who were sealed.
b) He saw the great crowd of the redeemed, from every nation, which could not be counted.
(*Note*: God knows the number of His servants, but no man does.)

DAY 7   a) They have been cleansed from sin by the blood of Christ, and have remained true even in the face of suffering.
b) They can (even now) worship and serve the Lord, have His protection, not lack anything, have Jesus as their shepherd.
c) There was silence in heaven.

GUIDE TO STUDY 5

DAY 1   a) They were crying out for justice to be done on the wicked; in Exodus it was also for deliverance from slavery.
b) Prayer: pleasing to God, a sweet fragrance. Smoke goes upwards; prayer ascends continually.

DAY 2   a) Partial, with only one third destroyed.
b) God speaks to people through His trumpet warnings. We can pray that people will hear Him and repent.

DAY 3   a) Satan (Luke 10:18; Isa. 13:12).
b) The abyss, or bottomless pit (Luke 8:31).
c) Those who do not have the seal of God on their foreheads.
d) Because they refused to respond to the mighty works of God.

DAY 4   a) The horsemen brought death. The locusts tortured but did not kill.
b) No.
c) That God is warning men of His wrath against sin, and giving them an opportunity to repent.
d) Personal.

DAY 5   a) The gospel.
b) Eat the scroll, and prophesy (proclaim God's message).
c) Because many people would not accept the gospel.

DAY 6   a) They will proclaim the gospel for a long but limited time;
b) Their power comes from the Holy Spirit; they have the powers Moses and Elijah had; they (the church) will go under and seem to perish at the end of the gospel age for a brief time (three and a half days) but will rise again to meet the Lord.
c) Revelation 11:2, 7-10.

DAY 7   a) Eternity.
b) 'Who is to come' is omitted in verse 17 as future time does not exist in eternity.
c) Because God's offer of mercy is no longer open (Luke 16:27-31).

Bring the music suggested in the Notes, if you can.

GUIDE TO STUDY 6

DAY I
a) First, the nation of Israel, then the new Israel, the church.
b) The Lord Jesus.
c) Satan.

DAY 2
a) When Christ was on earth.
b) By the blood of Jesus, their testimony and a martyr's heart.

DAY 3
a) His throne, his power and his authority.
b) Political power of a state opposed to God.

DAY 4
a) It was like a lamb; people worshipped it; it did miraculous signs; it was wounded but it lived; it could communicate to man; its followers were marked.
b) Many suggestions have been made: Communism, sects, witchcraft, other religions etc.

DAY 5
a) They are with the Lamb on Mount Zion; they have His name on their foreheads; they sing a new song; they have kept themselves pure (note that the idea of virginity is symbolic, pure for the Lord); they follow the Lamb; they have been made perfect.
b) Message of grace: the basic gospel to the world.
Message of doom: to the world system in rebellion against God.
Message of warning and personal challenge.

DAY 6
a) The harvest at the end of the age (Matt. 13:39).
b) Personal.
c) There is only one basis for assurance: faith in the finished work of Christ (Eph. 2:8, 9).

DAY 7
a) Because just as God delivered His people from slavery in Egypt, so the Lord Jesus brings deliverance to those who are slaves to sin.
b) He is Lord, King, almighty, just, true and holy.

GUIDE TO STUDY 7

DAY 1
a) Fear of a holy and awesome God, who punishes disobedience with death.
b) Pure linen of the angels; bowls filled with the wrath of God; and the fact that no one could enter until the plagues were ended.

DAY 2
a) Personal.
b) Because He has power to kill and cast into hell.
c) Because, though a person may get away with sin in this life, yet he still has to face the living God after death.

DAY 3
a) The Philistines were healed of the tumors after they sent the ark back. Exodus 7:20, 21; Revelation 8:8.

DAY 4
a) The wicked, who shed the blood of saints, had blood to drink.
b) The souls of the martyrs who, in an earlier vision, had cried out for judgment and justice.

DAY 5
a) The effect of the trumpets is partial, the bowls total.
b) They cursed God.
c) They refused to repent.

DAY 6
a) The evil spirits persuaded them with miraculous signs.
b) Christians have nothing to fear. Their Lord will come and their future is secure.
c) Be ready; live holy and godly lives; be on the alert.

DAY 7
a) To the total end of heaven and earth as we know them.
b) Jesus was referring to His work of redemption.
c) That they will receive a kingdom that cannot be shaken.

GUIDE TO STUDY 8

DAY 1
a) She has worshipped other gods and caused others to do the same.
b) She has the kings of earth in her power; the evil dragon is the one who supports her; she is adorned with gold and precious stones; she is drunk with the blood of saints.
c) Personal.

DAY 2
a) * One who has authority, leadership, strength and power.
b) Lord of lords, King of kings, victorious.
c) Whatever evil Satan can bring about, God can use to accomplish His purposes.

DAY 3
a) * God ordained it and it came as a judgment from Him.
b) Moral decay, greed for power, denial of God, etc.

DAY 4
a) Come out of her; rejoice because God has judged her.
b) The kings of the earth, the merchants and the seamen.

DAY 5
a) The stone sinks beneath the surface, and the civilisation is as though it had never been. No life!
b) Jerusalem.

DAY 6
a) Praise the Lord.
b) Because His judgment on Satan's activity in the world is just and right.
c) Those who serve Him and fear Him.

DAY 7
a) Her dress is pure linen; she is clothed in righteousness; she is the Lamb's bride, not in opposition to Him.
b) Christians must work out their salvation, living their lives to please God – yet salvation is a free gift from Him.

*Note: Babylon in this chapter is greater than any single city. She is the personification of humanist society. God's judgment will fall on any society which usurps the place of God and oppresses people who worship Him.

GUIDE TO STUDY 9

DAY 1 a) The Lord Jesus.
Faithful and True, the Word of God, King of Kings and Lord of Lords.
b) No time is mentioned.

DAY 2 a) The birds gather, knowing that the kings will soon be dead.
b) To a wedding banquet prepared by the King for His Son.

DAY 3 a) The beast from the sea, the beast from the earth, the beast on which the woman sat.
b) Satan's world power.
c) At the end of the age.

DAY 4 a) The parable of the strong man is the only other reference to the binding of Satan. It was told to illustrate what happened to Satan when someone stronger came to earth and began casting out demons.
b) It was only when Christ came that the good news was preached to non Jews. Until then, Satan had deceived them. See Genesis 22:18; Isaiah 9:2, 6; Luke 2:30; Acts 2:5.
c) Personal.

DAY 5 a) Passing from death to life, which may refer to being born again.
b) Revelation 16:14-16; 17:14; 19:19-21.

DAY 6 a) According to what they have done.
b) By Christ's righteousness (Isa. 61:10).
c) In the book of life.
d) Hebrews 9:27.

DAY 7 a) God will live with them; there will be no more death, crying or pain; they will receive the water of life.
b) Alpha, the Beginning: He was before the world was created.
  Omega, the End: He continues for ever.

GUIDE TO STUDY 10

DAY 1 a) The church.
b) He is building His church, making us holy by the study of His Word.
c) It shines with the glory of God.

DAY 2 a) It has the names of the twelve tribes of Israel and the twelve apostles.
b) The city is measured, and every metre accounted for. Revelation: precious stones, pearls, gold.
c) Isaiah: garments of salvation, robe of righteousness, bridegroom.

DAY 3 a) The temple was a meeting place of God and man. But just to be part of the heavenly city is to be with Him.
b) God is light, and His glory pervades everything.
c) Nothing impure will be allowed in.

DAY 4 a) In Revelation it is a garden within a city; leaves for healing rather than a fall into sin; water of life; the throne of God; the curse removed; servants are obedient; no need for the sun.

DAY 5 a) The God of the spirits of the prophets (NIV), or who gives His Spirit to the prophets (GNB).
b) Because God spoke to man through His Son.

DAY 6 a) It will be a permanent state of righteousness or unrighteousness.
b) They have been forgiven and made clean through Christ's sacrifice.
c) Personal.
Having eternal life is the only reason (John 3:16).

DAY 7 a) The water of life.
b) Personal.
c) God will bring eternal punishment upon him.

THE WORD WORLDWIDE

We first heard of WORD WORLDWIDE over twenty years ago when Marie Dinnen, its founder, shared excitedly about the wonderful way ministry to one needy woman had exploded to touch many lives. It was great to see the Word of God being made central in the lives of thousands of men and women, then to witness the life-changing results of them applying the Word to their circumstances. Over the years the vision for WORD WORLDWIDE has not dimmed in the hearts of those who are involved in this ministry. God is still at work through His Word and in today's self-seeking society, the Word is even more relevant to those who desire true meaning and purpose in life. WORD WORLDWIDE is a ministry of WEC International, an interdenominational missionary society, whose sole purpose is to see Christ known, loved and worshipped by all, particularly those who have yet to hear of His wonderful name. This ministry is a vital part of our work and we warmly recommend the WORD WORLDWIDE 'Geared for Growth' Bible studies to you. We know that as you study His Word you will be enriched in your personal walk with Christ. It is our hope that as you are blessed through these studies, you will find opportunities to help others discover a personal relationship with Jesus. As a mission we would encourage you to work with us to make Christ known to the ends of the earth.

Stewart and Jean Moulds – British Directors, **WEC International.**

A full list of over 50 'Geared for Growth' studies can be obtained from:

John and Ann Edwards
5 Louvaine Terrace, Hetton-le-Hole, Tyne & Wear, DH5 9PP
Tel. 0191 5262803 Email: rhysjohn.edwards@virgin.net

Anne Jenkins
2 Windermere Road, Carnforth, Lancs., LA5 9AR
Tel. 01524 734797 Email: anne@jenkins.abelgratis.com

UK Website: www.gearedforgrowth.co.uk

OLD TESTAMENT

Triumphs Over Failures: A Study in Judges ISBN 1-85792-888-1 (above left)
Messenger of Love: A Study in Malachi ISBN 1-85792-885-7 (above right)
The Beginning of Everything: A Study in Genesis 1-11 ISBN 0-90806-728-3
Hypocrisy in Religion: A Study in Amos ISBN 0-90806-706-2
Unshakeable Confidence: A Study in Habakkuk & Joel ISBN 0-90806-751-8
A Saviour is Promised: A Study in Isaiah 1 - 39 ISBN 0-90806-755-0
Our Magnificent God: A Study in Isaiah 40 - 66 ISBN 1-85792-909-8
The Throne and Temple: A Study in 1 & 2 Chronicles ISBN 1-85792-910-1
The Cost of Obedience: A Study in Jeremiah ISBN 0-90806-761-5
Focus on Faith: A Study of 10 Old Testament Characters ISBN 1-85792-890-3
Faith, Courage and Perserverance: A Study in Ezra ISBN 1-85792-949-7
Amazing Love: A Study in Hosea ISBN 1-84550-004-0

NEW TESTAMENT

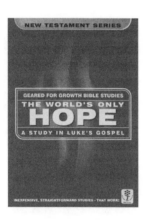

The World's Only Hope: A Study in Luke ISBN 1-85792-886-5 (above left)
Walking in Love: A Study in John's Epistles ISBN 1-85792-891-1 (above right)
Faith that Works: A Study in James ISBN 0-90806-701-1
Made Completely New: A Study in Colossians & Philemon ISBN 0-90806-721-6
Jesus-Christ, Who is He? A Study in John's Gospel ISBN 0-90806-716-X
Entering by Faith: A Study in Hebrews ISBN 1-85792-914-4
Heavenly Living: A Study in Ephesians ISBN 1-85792-911-X
The Early Church: A Study in Acts 1-12 ISBN 0-90806-736-4
Worldwide Evangelization: A Study in Acts 13-28 ISBN 1-84550-005-9
Get Ready: A Study in 1 & 2 Thessalonians ISBN 1-85792-948-9
Glimpses of the King: A Study in Matthew's Gospel ISBN 1-84550-007-5
Born to be Free: A Study in Galatians ISBN 1-84550-019-9
Controlled by Love: A Study in 2 Corinthians ISBN 1-84550-022-9
People and Problems in the Church: A Study in 1st Corinthians
ISBN 1-84550-021-0

CHARACTER

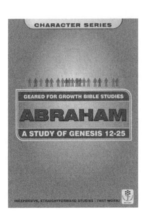 

Abraham: A Study of Genesis 12-25 ISBN 1-85792-887-3 (above left)
Serving the Lord: A Study of Joshua ISBN 1-85792-889-X (above right)
Achieving the Impossible: A Study of Nehemiah ISBN 0-90806-707-0
God plans for Good: A Study of Joseph ISBN 0-90806-700-3
A Man After God's Own Heart: A Study of David ISBN 0-90806-746-1
Grace & Grit: A Study of Ruth & Esther ISBN 1-85792-908-X
Men of Courage: A Study of Elijah & Elisha ISBN 1-85792-913-6
Meek but Mighty: A Study of Moses ISBN 1-85792-951-9
Highly Esteemed: A Study of Daniel ISBN 1-84550-006-7
A Man with a Choice: A Study in the Life of Solomon ISBN 1-84550-023-7
God Cares: A Study in the Life of Jonah ISBN 1-84550-024-5
The Man God Chose: A Study in the Life of Jacob ISBN 1-84550-025-3

THEMES

God's Heart, My Heart: World Mission ISBN 1-85792-892-X (above left)
Freedom: You Can Find it! ISBN 0-90806-702-X (above right)
Freely Forgiven: A Study in Redemption ISBN 0-90806-720-8
The Problems of Life! Is there an Answer? ISBN 1-85792-907-1
Understanding the Way of Salvation ISBN 0-90082-880-3
Saints in Service: 12 Bible Characters ISBN 1-85792-912-8
Finding Christ in the Old Testament: Pre-existence and Prophecy
ISBN 0-90806-739-9

Christian Focus Publications

publishes books for all ages

Our mission statement –

STAYING FAITHFUL

In dependence upon God we seek to help make His infallible word, the Bible, relevant. Our aim is to ensure that the Lord Jesus Christ is presented as the only hope to obtain forgiveness of sin, live a useful life and look forward to heaven with Him.

REACHING OUT

Christ's last command requires us to reach out to our world with His gospel. We seek to help fulfil that by publishing books that point people towards Jesus and help them develop a Christ-like maturity. We aim to equip all levels of readers for life, work, ministry and mission.

Books in our adult range are published in three imprints.

Christian Focus contains popular works including biographies, commentaries, basic doctrine, and Christian living. Our children's books are also published in this imprint.

Mentor focuses on books written at a level suitable for Bible College and seminary students, pastors, and other serious readers; the imprint includes commentaries, doctrinal studies, examination of current issues, and church history.

Christian Heritage contains classic writings from the past.

For details of our titles visit us on our website
www.christianfocus.com

Christian Focus Publications Ltd
Geanies House, Fearn, Tain,
Ross-shire, IV20 ITW, Scotland, United Kingdom.
info@christianfocus.com